I0486955

The PowerZone Sales System
Align and Conquer!

Unlocking the potential
power of people, products and markets

BY FRANK P. DEFINA

Dedication

To my wife Patricia, sons Frank and James for their constant feedback and support as I developed the Power-Zone concepts. To my father who instilled in me the basic principles of selling as I observed him in his own business and who taught me the meaning of true customer service. To mom, who kept us smiling with her incredible pasta dishes.

Acknowledgement

Many of the fundamentals incorporated in this book came from my sales mentor; Samuel H. Liptak. A remarkable yet unassuming leader, manager, and friend who forged the foundation of my successful sales career. Sam understood the "person" part of salesperson better than anyone. He knew that it was important that he believe in me which led to believing in myself.

Throughout my career there have been many people who have contributed to my ongoing sales education and who have provided inspiration, support, leadership, opportunity, and friendship. Special thanks to Jerry Steiner, Rick Albert, Bill Haus, Jay Delostretto, Scott Watson, Bob Klein, Rusty Vernon, Jim Jagodinski, Steve Yuhas, Bob Garino, Andy Hori, Bob Mueller, Scott Mimura, Peggy Wolenski, Terry Yokoyama, Vince Galdi, Fred Goldberger, Joe Greenfeld, Eli Katz, Mike Duncan, John Galliard, Todd Yui, Wendy Diddel, Dave Smith, Doyle Ledford, Brian James, Robert Levin, Jean-Pierre Trebot, Futoshi Umeki, Alex Nogami, Bo Polatty, Julianna Benedick, Keith Ridings, Yuji Hirota, Kaz Kamijo, Patricia Torelli, Ted Conboy, Nori Kaneko, Dick Pasterchick, Tom Zitelli, Yoonho Ha, Jin Whan Ahn, finally to Don Spradling; one of the best presenters I've ever encountered and who was the first person to use the term PowerZone during a formal presentation.

About the Author

Frank P. De Fina was born near Pittsburgh, PA where he started his career as a field salesperson eventually assuming a District Sales Manager position with Panasonic Corporation of North America. In the next 26 years he held numerous positions at Panasonic including Product Manager; Digital Cameras, National Sales Manager; Professional Video, Vice-President; Medical Imaging , President; Video Security Systems, and President; Broadcast & Television Systems. He was named President, Panasonic Systems Solutions Company of America in 1999.

He holds a B.S. in Business Administration and a M.S. in Communications from Clarion, University of Pennsylvania, and completed additional graduate programs in Finance and Sales management at the University of Pennsylvania, Wharton School of Business.   Mr. De Fina also studied International Business at the Matsushita Institute for Learning, Hirakata, Japan.

He serves on the boards of the New York Friar's Club Foundation and The Paley Center for Media in New York City. He is also on the Executive Boards of the Security Industry Association and the International Biometrics Association. An avid collector of vintage guitars and amplifiers he currently lives near Princeton, NJ with his wife Patricia and their two collies, Max and Baliegh.

Email: Frank@powerzoneselling.com
Blog: blog.powerzoneselling.com
Web Page: www.powerzoneselling.com

The PowerZone Sales System
Align and Conquer!

(Unlocking the potential power of people, products and markets)

Introduction

This book is intended to be read in a short time such as on a cross country flight or in a single afternoon. Points are made quickly with maximum emphasis on immediate implementation. Whether you are brand new to sales or an experienced sales professional my hope is that you can benefit from its succinct approach to organization of your sales effort. This is not another 'how to sell'' treatise but rather, "how to organize your sales activity to achieve results".

What is a PowerZone?

DeFinaData:
Every person, product, service, distributor, customer, application, competitor, manager, CEO *has, is, or can become* **a PowerZone.**

Everyone does something well. My mother makes wonderful Italian food, consistently great, every time with no exceptions. That's her *PowerZone*. Ichiro Suzuki is one of the best hitters to ever play in the major leagues, consistent hitting is his *PowerZone*. Ronald Reagan's *PowerZone* was his gift of communicating complex issues. The local mechanic's *PowerZone*? He can instantly tell what's ailing my car's engine from a brief test drive. What's your *PowerZone*? Your company's? What one or two strong attributes do you rely on when facing adversity? Which of your company's products sells consistently well? Why do your customers buy certain products from you and others from your competitors? *PowerZones!*

But no one is good at everything. While my mom makes great veal dishes, I don't see her cakes as a threat to Betty Crocker. Suzuki, fabulous hitter-but few home runs. Reagan never won an academy award. Perhaps you can drive a golf ball nearly 300 yards but still cannot hit a good sand wedge. Coca-Cola strayed from their *PowerZone*; "Classic Coke" but quickly returned to it when "New Coke" produced sagging sales. McDonald's sells billions of hamburgers but failed to successfully launch the McRib.

All companies face this fundamental *PowerZone Dilemma*: *some products seemingly sell themselves while others sleep soundly in the warehouse.*

Enterprises need to maximize current sales and create sustainable sales growth. With limited selling time, how do we leverage the most powerful aspects of the sales offering? Products, services, salespeople, managers, channels, markets, all have individual *PowerZone Attributes or variables*. Features, service models, construction quality are attributes that can be quantified on a ratings scale. Throughout our study, we'll constantly assess the attributes of our *PowerZone Variables;* people, product features, service levels, sales channels, are examples, and, you'll identify your own products' *PZ Variables*. Additionally, we'll assign a ranking number or *PowerZone Value* to help us focus on the most important aspects.

DeFinaData:
While no product is perfect, every product has at least one market, one application, and some price point where it will sell effectively. This is the product's fundamental PowerZone.

The concept of *PowerZones* applied to the sales process is the focus of this book. By identifying *PowerZones* through careful analysis and then *aligning* your organization's strategy to leverage these advantages you'll be able to increase your sales by focusing on strengths and avoiding areas that lead to failure. We'll learn how to chart these attributes, assigning numerical value to them and then mapping these, finally aligning the strongest attributes to create your individual *PowerZone sales strategy;* a strategy that will guide your weekly planning and daily sales activity. *PowerZones* work best when product, people, market, support, infrastructure, and marketing are aligned and coordinated.

In subsequent chapters, we'll create the *PowerZone Matrix* which will assess your company's PZ and then direct your sales and marketing activities. We'll also chart your *competitor's PowerZones* in an exercise designed to help you avoid their strengths while attacking their weaknesses.

I don't intend to write a lengthy treatise so we'll hit the key concepts quickly and then apply the principles to your own situation. At the end of the process you'll have a good idea of where and how to sell your products successfully. Most important, you'll create your own individual *PowerZone Matrix* which becomes the action plan for your sales effort!

If you sell products, systems, services, or manage sales teams, this book is for you. As a salesperson and sales executive for the past 30 years, I've seen great salespeople do wonderful things with products that were-just like yours- very good but never perfect. I've observed many times how one person could exceed their sales targets consistently month after month while others with the same product would struggle. During my own career as a field sales person, sales team leader, and company president (actually a combination of all three functions); I've worked the sales process daily and have experienced nearly every example within this text also making many mistakes as I learned how to organize the sales effort. I've also led teams to astounding success in highly competitive markets with products that were good and often great but never having every feature nor ever offered at the lowest market price.

Accept this fact- while you will never be selling a 100% best in *all categories* product, you can successfully sell *any* product or service by applying a *PowerZone Strategy* based on principles presented here.

Although I did not realize it at the time, the *PowerZone* process was developing over many years largely through personal necessity! In the late '70s as a young salesperson with little sales training I was thrown into a highly competitive market selling broadcast television systems. My company's products were very good, in fact, as an authorized reseller for various manufacturers, I could choose from a variety of solutions. The real problems for me were fundamental. Which customers should I approach? How to present my products? How should my weekly schedule be organized?

You can very easily be overwhelmed by sales managers, quota pressures, and the personal drive that led you to a sales career. If you consider the *actual selling time* available during normal business hours, it is easy to conclude that you must absolutely maximize those precious moments.

DeFinaData:
The number one mission of sales management should be *organization* of the sales effort in order to *exceed* the company's goals.
Your manager must clearly understand your own sales plan and help you to succeed. It is this organizational aspect of the sales process that is most critical.

DeFinaData:
Meeting goals is our commitment as salespeople. It is the minimum acceptable performance. Sales teams should be positioned to exceed goals!

As a beginning salesperson in the late 1970's I quickly understood the need to optimize selling time, focus on the most powerful aspects of my product, and concentrate on the customers with the highest probability for success. This was the need from which the *PowerZone* process was born. Over the next few decades, I would become very successful as both a salesperson and sales leader by applying these organizational principles.

It was during our company's 2004 National Sales Meeting ("Sales Camp") that the efficacy of *PowerZones* surfaced in a team environment. In fact, the entire meeting morphed into the very first **PowerZone Workshop** as I presented the company's strategy to our sales team!

We had just introduced a digital recorder for the security surveillance industry that could capture images from security cameras; recording and storing them for later retrieval. The sales team generally had been underperforming but some people were achieving outstanding sales. When I asked one of the successful salespeople, Steve, to stand and tell the others the secret to his excellent sales, he simply stated, "I focus on selling the recorder to schools since they have no access control system to connect to. Our recorder does not connect easily to an access control system."

If you are not familiar with "access control" it does not matter. The fact is, other salespeople were approaching the entire market as a whole and failing because the product did not connect to existing systems in the traditional installed base. As commentary to Steve's report I responded: "Steve has found a successful zone for the product, he's *aligned* or *directed* the product's most powerful features and strengths to solving the specific problems of a targeted market, he has found the product's *Power Zone!*"

As the conference continued I realized that *PowerZones* were easily applied to not only products but people, channels, market positioning, messaging, sales management, in fact, every aspect of the selling process. Others in the room had individual *PowerZones*. Even our dealers and channel partners were cited by the group as having *PowerZones* in different markets. This epiphany at the conference evolved into an organized, repeatable process that could be used to guide any sales force selling *any* product into *any* market.

During breakout sessions the team organized the sales strategy based upon *aligning PowerZones* of product, people, dealers, aiming at specific vertical markets where the product solved identified problems for customers.

DefinaData:
"<u>Problem solving is the key reason for selling success.</u> Products and services succeed when they solve customer's problems or enhance their lives."

Apple's *I-Pods* are everywhere because they were designed for a very focused demographic. They enhance the lives of music lovers by providing easy downloads from immense music libraries, storing and easily retrieving hundreds of the user's favorite tunes, *and*, solving the problem of conveniently taking the music anywhere. The Apple *I-Phone* is a brilliant concept which adds many features including mobile phone, internet, media management, and GPS. Apple is moving the world into a "single appliance society" where one device fulfills all communication needs. This is a powerful example of **PowerZone Alignment**.

Throughout this book we'll use examples from the business world and chart *PowerZones* while aligning them on a matrix chart. Similarly, we'll chart your products and service offerings creating your own map to maximize sales and dominate in your market. We've combined the words "power" and "zone" to place more emphasis on the concept as a cohesive process.

The PowerZone Formula:

$Pz+A=D$
To make the point early and often, we'll use this "equation" during our PowerZone journey:

PowerZone + Alignment = Dominance

The term *PowerZone* refers to a sales process- an *organizational principle* that uses the strengths of any product to determine its ideal customer. Alignment is the process by which we connect the strongest *PowerZones* into a focused and executable sales strategy. Likewise, the *PowerZone* process clearly outlines weaknesses in our product, channels, people, etc. as they relate to the selling process. Our competitors may have significant *PowerZones* that we want to avoid or develop countermeasures against. Their weaknesses in an area of our strongest *PowerZones* become essential attack elements of our sales team's presentation. As we develop the strategy and refine our sales effort to maximize our *PowerZones* we begin the process of dominating the targeted market niche. As we dominate in more niches we produce sustainable sales growth and commanding market share.

Pz+A=D   PowerZones, Aligned, lead to Dominance of a niche

PowerZoning (the actionable form of this process) is a *general systems approach* to the process of sales as a whole – a method for creating a foundation upon which a successful sales strategy can be built. The **PowerZone Matrix** is the map from which the strategy becomes evident; a working and dynamic action plan which is constantly updated and refined with current data from within your company and from the market in which you operate. This essentially becomes your living sales plan; maximizing your time and energy.

1

The Power Zone Concept

Incorporated into the training at Japanese companies the sales staff is taught some history; in the feudal period (1600-1868) the merchants of Osaka and Edo (now Tokyo) were careful not to sleep with their feet pointed in the direction of their steady customers so as to not commit the slightest disrespect to those people.

At the center of every long-term successful sales strategy is respect and appreciation for the customer:

Sales success is about *them*, not us!
How to reach *them*?
Who best to sell to *them*?
What trade magazines do *they* read?
Which channel is best for reaching *them*?

How do our products enhance *their* lives?
And vitally important, which of our products best solve *their* problems?

"Looking after one customer gains you one hundred."
Konosuke Matsushita (1894-1989)

From humble beginnings Konosuke Matsushita built one of the greatest electronics companies in the world; Panasonic. He did so in part by realizing how a company and the greater society can be understood as a large set of inter-relating and overlapping systems and how inattention to any of these can threaten the success of an organization.

DeFina Data:
The PowerZone System uses a general systems theory approach to the process of sales as a whole.

In PowerZone selling we systematically arrive at our strategy, align the most powerful attributes, and then execute to grow sales and dominate our market niche.

This general systems approach has had enormous impact in the study of organizations; the concept of "systems" is familiar to most. But here we present systematic thinking as the key to sales strategy. The application of systems thinking has been incorporated into the language commonly used to describe the everyday world: a car's electrical system, the health care system, bodily systems, family systems, political systems, educational systems, financial systems, information systems, and so on.

This approach is invaluable because the sheer amount of information available on virtually everything has increased exponentially during the past century, and the rate of increase seems to be speeding up rather than slowing down. We can never know all there is to know, so we seek some way of organizing what we encounter – both to avoid missing essential information and to avoid being overloaded.

As sales professionals we are inundated by different systems and we must gain some basic understanding of what these systems are and how they work.

"Systems thinking is based on the fundamental shift of perception from the world as a machine to the world as a living system." – Fritjof Capra

DeFina Data:
We can be more effective as individuals and help create a more successful business if we approach the day-to-day practice of selling with a more sophisticated awareness of the processes that contribute to that success.

A Little Green Plastic Army Sales Force

When I was a kid, among my favorite toys was an enormous box of little green plastic army men, along with numerous tanks, pillboxes, and small plastic barbed-wire fences. Acquired over a number of holidays and birthdays, occasional trips to the toy store and a few swaps with my friends, I'd amassed quite an army in my closet. I played with them in the back yard by the edge of some woods where I could create elaborate battle scenarios. I would take the box and dump it out onto the ground. Imagine the general chaos of that scene; the toys fell from the box landing on their sides, pointing their rifles at each other, seemingly ready to throw grenades into their own ranks. All the individual elements I'd used to create my invincible invading force were initially one big jumbled mess.

Now, don't misunderstand my green army men metaphor – I am not about to quote from Sun Tzu's *The Art of War* and I don't necessarily think it's useful to see the sales process through a militaristic prism – but I do see each and every toy soldier lying in the grass as *representing some individual random element in the various systems of sales.*

DeFina Data:
It is the purpose of the PowerZone System to identify and align, in a structured, time-efficient and logical manner, all the important segments, both people and product that represent an unstoppable team.

The Vital "Publics"

A significant key to the *PowerZone* approach to sales is in the identification and proper alignment of all the vital "publics". "Publics" is not a word you are accustomed to seeing in its plural form, but understanding the value of *publics* is important to the task at hand.

Think of an organization.

Think of the last school you attended.

Think of the electronics retailer nearest your house.

Think of the non-profit food bank in your community.

Think of the local shopping mall.

Think of the F.B.I.

Think of your own company.

Before I got involved in what has became a successful career in electronics sales, my background was in media, film and television production. When I think of *publics*, I think of them in the way that a producer of media might think of *audiences*.

Messages should always be designed with specific *population characteristics* in mind, whether they are designed to sell a product or your organization. Likewise, your approach to selling should include careful analysis of your own *publics*, distilling them down to the most applicable targets for your sales activity.

We will examine some of the principles and techniques of *audience analysis* employed in various settings. The goal here is not to become adept at audience research;

the goal here more resembles a sort of pragmatic scavenging. We will borrow from all sorts of places like media theory, systems theory, communication theory, marketing and advertising research, looking for things that apply. The selection criterion is simple and straightforward: does it make our job easier and more efficient? If the answer is "no" we discard it; if the answer is "yes" then it goes into the *PowerZone* matrix.

DeFina Data:
The way to approach this concept of *publics* is to consider that you are almost always dealing with both *internal* and *external* publics.

Who are the internal publics?

The *internal publics* are found in the way that any organization breaks itself down into smaller units, defined most commonly by function.

As a sales person you are most likely familiar with situations where your relationship with a customer was jeopardized because of the action (or inaction) of another unit within your own organization. These internal publics may include upper management who set the quotas, engineers/technical support staff who will service your customer's pre-and-post-sale, an accounting/billing department who understands whatever arrangement you made with a customer (or who must make clear to you the specific arrangements that are possible) as well as employees representing other internal publics with whom there will be some type of interaction at any given point during the sales process.

Some of these internal publics can be *PowerZones.* A responsive credit department or a highly efficient logistics system can have dramatic effect on your sales. Always consider your internal publics in the analysis of your organization.

Who are the external publics?

The population of individuals and organizations that represent the primary market for your product represent the *external publics,* i.e.; the audiences you will, in effect, be hoping to attract. To a large degree, *external publics* are determined by the specifics of your products and company.

If everybody everywhere bought just one of whatever it is you're selling your parking space in the company lot would most probably improve. It is nonetheless a mistake to answer the question: "Who is my audience?" with a simple "well… everybody."

Sales are never quite that simple.
Let's consider a quick service restaurant like *McDonald's.* Think about the systems involved, and examine those in human terms.

First, their *internal publics:*
The first division is one of line employees and supervisors. A restaurant's employees will be made up of full

and part-time workers and supervisors (a manager and assistant managers.) From a manager or franchise owner's perspective, employees can be arranged in terms of seniority, dependability, education, training and so on.

There are also systems of supply – purveyors of everything from napkins, condiments, produce, kitchen supplies, uniforms, and cleaning supplies, as well as the companies who supply complex software for ordering and cash registers (actually, POS "point of sale" systems that are more like powerful small computers).

Next, the systems of support – companies responsible for printing paper placemats, table tents, coupons; local and regional advertisers; companies who maintain and repair all the various cooking and refrigeration equipment.

You can correctly assume that McDonald's Corp. has a great many *PowerZones* in terms of *internal publics*, one of many reasons that they maintain a dominate position in the quick service restaurant industry. Even vendors are considered as *PowerZones* and cherished as *McDonald's* team members.

There are no more important and essential *external publics* than customers. Not only does "looking after one customer gain you one hundred," so too may losing one customer lose many. Other *external publics* include *competing* fast food establishments in the *McDonald's* space. In one city in the Midwest, a third place burger restaurant moved into first place after responding to a growing Hispanic population by wisely hiring bi-lingual counter workers and placing a few signs in Spanish on display; steps none of their competitors had taken.

The lesson here is that *PowerZones* must be continuously honed; refined, revisited, attended to, if the PZ premise is to remain viable for your company. Maintaining an ongoing equilibrium among a complex network of inter-relating systems is central to success. A manager of a fast food franchise must be concerned with maintaining sales figures at or above a certain level. Removed from the specifics of French fries and diet soft drinks, the general principles at work in the survival and success of a small one-owner sandwich shop or a multi-national corporation can be approached in the same way.

DeFina Data:
This systematic approach to any organization and specific sales situation is what the Power Zone System uses to build its foundation.

Here's a quick exercise. Consider *your* organization.

a. List three *systems* (departments or functions) essential to your sales effort.

b. List three **internal** publics.

c. List three **external** publics.

d. Within the three **internal** publics, select one and further divide it into as many sub sections as you can

e. Do the same for one of your **external** publics.

This exercise will begin to train your mind to think in terms of PowerZone Attributes which populate your PZ Matrix.

2

Mapping the Territory

DeFina Data:
Given the most essential components, the actual *practice* of sales has not changed all that much since our great-grandparent's day. What has changed is the level of sophistication that we bring to our understanding of that practice.

Nominated for six Academy Awards in 1962, Meredith Wilson's *The Music Man* opens with a scene inside of a rail road car full of traveling salesmen. During that scene one of the salesmen repeats at least three or four times what, for him, is the key to success or failure in his trade:

"You gotta know the *territory!*"

True. The territory or space we operate in must be totally understood. But essential to that understanding is the continued analysis of the territory as a system of end-users, dealers, distributors, consumers.

Somewhere within that system are the *PowerZones* for your product. Within your sales territory are the problems that your product solves. Important components of the system are your sales force, internal, and external publics. We'll need to plot these *PZ variables* as we uncover and dissect them in terms of *PowerZones*. Again, we must align them in order to reach our own sales strategy.

DeFina Data:
The concept of *alignment* is the critical component in the Power Zone System.

In order to deliver a successful product to the marketplace, you must identify and align the systems that you're working with.

Approaching Audience Analysis and Population Characteristics

Imagine you're on a flight somewhere over the North Atlantic and the passenger in the seat next to you is suddenly taken ill. There is no emergency room on the flight; there are no diagnostic tools, no expensive medical equipment. Even so, it's more likely that a physician would be able to make a determination of the seriousness of the situation, whether it's necessary to turn the flight around or divert it to the nearest air-port. Why?

"Because she's a doctor, she's been to medical school." Yes, but that's not the most basic explanation. The physician is able to approach a situation that you or I would see as little more than chaos – a person thrashing about, out of control – because the physician possesses a template that can be used to overlay some structure, to force some *sense of order on that chaos.*

On the most basic level, the doctor considering the sick person is no different than a trained mechanic opening the hood of your car and listening to that awful noise it's just started to make. And the mechanic is no dif-ferent than the pro golfer considering a particularly dif-ficult shot on the 5th hole at Pebble Beach. Where you or I might poke the passenger in the abdomen and ask if it hurts; or reach in and jiggle a spark plug wire for no particular reason; the person with an understanding of the systems involved will approach the situation with a general plan of attack.

DeFina Data:
The Power Zone sales professional will be able to approach equally chaotic situations and impose a sense of order on the chaos.

Audience analysis, (the use of population characteristics) is one important tool at your disposal. In broad terms, an audience – in this case, a population of potential cus-tomers – can be examined in *quantitative* and *qualitative* terms. We most often associate notions of "audience research" with quantitative methods, usually population characteristics expressed through statistical data in the form of *demographics*. Some of this information is essential when making decisions regarding the communication with potential customers. Don't be concerned about the academic nature of this discussion; we're setting our sights on the *PowerZone* attributes of our customers.

Basic statistical data — average age, gender, ethnicity, income, education, —can give you an important edge in crafting a successful approach;

Are you approaching an organization?
Who in the organization will be influencing purchasing recommendations?
Who will make purchasing decisions?
Who holds the key to achieving sales that are not immediately apparent?
How thoroughly can you describe these people?
Do you know enough about them to prepare an effective message?

Practical Applications

Most of the time you will not be caught up in the sort of long and detailed marketing analysis that requires the hiring of an outside market research firm and the preparation of detailed statistical analyses of a target population. Most of the time you will be working within tight time constraints and left to your own resources.

Understanding some basic concepts and processes of quantitative and qualitative audience research methods will make it possible for you to develop a thumbnail sketch of your situation that can help impose some necessary order on the chaos.

"The map is not the territory." – Alfred Korzybski (Doctor of Metaphysical Science)

Quantitative methods are those which deal in quantities, things that can be counted, numbered, averaged, etc. Quantitative methods are essentially *reductionistic*. This means that they reduce extremely complex phenomena into columns of numbers. It is important that you remain aware of the pitfalls of this approach. We're not doing any math here; rather we are applying this approach to reach a fairly detailed map of our sales strategy.

As we map *PZ Variables* such as features, ease of operation, flavor, whatever, we'll need to assign numerical value; ranking them based on there relative power. A PZ value of "5" (PZ5) represents the most powerful attribute while a PZ value of "1" (PZ1) represents the least powerful or least compelling attribute.

How would you answer the following question?

You are faced with an imaginary life/death situation and asked to answer three questions to save your life. You must answer all three questions correctly to survive. However, you get to choose the subject matter.

What subject would you choose?

If you answered, "history", for instance, you have identified your personal PowerZone for general knowledge. We would assign a PZ5 *value* designation to the *PowerZoneVariable*, "history". In fact we can say that "history" is the **primary PowerZone**. If you are also quite knowledgeable about geography, this is also a PowerZone albeit not the *primary PowerZone* so we may assign a PZ4 designation here.

History and Geography are now plotted (on our PZ Matrix) in the "5" and "4" columns which identify our *primary* and *secondary PowerZone variables* for that category.

PowerZone Matrix   "Life and Death Exercise"

	Insignificant	Low	Marginal	Secondary PowerZone	Primary PowerZone	
	PZI	**PZ2**	**PZ3**	**PZ4**	**PZ5**	
Subject Matter	Horticulture	French cooking	Baseball Stats	Geography	History	

In this imaginary exercise, we've listed "baseball stats", "French cooking", and horticulture" as PZ3, PZ2, and PZI respectively. Your products may also map similarly. You'll have one significant product feature that is the most compelling and that becomes PZ5. Also, you may have features that are strong but which many competitors equal, exceed, or that may be less significant. These are PZ3, PZ2, or PZ1.

As another simple example, think of your best product and rank its most compelling features:

We'll use an imaginary digital surveillance camera.

PZ5 **picture quality.**
PZ4 **reliability.**
PZ3 **day/night usage.**
PZ2 **connectivity to existing systems.**
PZ1 **low price**

Now rank your salespeople from most knowledgeable to least knowledgeable regarding their technical and presentation abilities for this product:

These are fictitious names but you get the point.
PZ5 **Frank Mace** (your best salesperson, proven sales record in this category)
PZ4 **Amy Masterson** (very good but slightly less experienced in this product)
PZ3 **Deepak Patel** (promising beginner with good technical grasp, minimal experience)
PZ2 **Morris Lanisette** (struggles with this type of digital technology)
PZ1 **Mark Abramson** (not suitable for selling this level of product)

Now indicate which *applications* you rank as most likely targets given the features and other variables for this product:

PZ5 **Parking Lots** (they need reliable cameras that produce high quality images in both day and night)

PZ4 **School Playgrounds** (same requirements but mostly daytime usage).

PZ3 **Casinos** (Maybe, but they have good lighting in doors so may not pay for day/night features they don't need)

PZ2 **Convenience Stores** (Traditionally very low quality is enough, mainly use cameras as deterrent to shoplifting).

PZI **Churches and Synagogues** (most likely using cameras for broadcasting rather than surveillance)

In this example, the PZ *variables* and corresponding PZ *values* have, been studied and carefully plotted validating as many assumptions as possible. Applying very simple *alignment,* the sales of this product would be maximized if salespeople PZ5 and PZ4 focused on *applications* rated at PZ5 and PZ4 or customers where the feature variables provided the best solution.

As we *PowerZone* the digital camera example the simple PZ Matrix might look like this:

PowerZone Matrix "Digital Surveillance Cameras"

	Insignificant	Low Significance	Marginal	Secondary	Primary
PZ Variable	PZ1	PZ2	PZ3	PZ4	PZ5
Features	Price	connectivity	Day/Night Capable	Reliability	Picture Quality
Salesperson.	Abramson	Green	Patel	Masterson	Mace
Application	Churches and Synagogues	C-Stores	Casinos	School Playgrounds	Parking Lots

Although many more variables would need to be studied and charted, in this example, it appears that salespersons Mace and Masterson would likely succeed in selling this product by focusing the sales effort on schools and commercial parking lots.

So imagine yourself before this exercise. Would you have presented the camera to churches and convenience stores in your territory? Probably, and you would spend a great deal of precious sales time on applications where this camera is not the best solution. So given four possible sales calls in one day, would you not be more likely to succeed by calling on four parking lots rather than four churches?

You may have guessed that a key *PZ variable* may be specific applications or customer types. If you sell high performance automobiles then PZ5 above may be "zero to 60" and PZ4 could be "sport suspension". Mary O'Malley may be your PZ5 salesperson based on her mastering of the PZ5 and PZ4 features.

There is no list of *PZ variables* that apply universally. You'll need to identify the pertinent ones for your product and plot them on your own matrix. This type of study works well in a group setting.

DefinaData:
Consensus within a sales team is a strong indicator of validation when determining *PZ variables* and *PZ values*.

I urge you to use the team or workshop approach when feasible. The risk of missing key publics, variables, attributes, competitive PZs is greatly diminished and your PZ matrix will be more effective.

The point here is to spend time getting good quality information as you plot items on your PZ Matrix. Validate the information and update it often. A little extra effort during the information gathering stage will reap great benefits in terms of sales. Poor quality data input will lead to ineffective strategy. This is not a good place to make invalid assumptions. Be sure to carefully confirm your conclusions as to PZ variables and their relative strength. If you have 500 lines of resolution on your camera but your competitors all have 700 lines you may not want to assign a PZ5 to "resolution". You'll need to find a more compelling PZ5 such as "virtually indestructible" which when aligned with other variables may lead you to an entirely different strategy.

Our *internal* and *external publics* would need *PZ value* assessment as well.

Posing these questions leads to identification of the compelling *PZ variables*.

Again, study the publics; identify PZ Variables and the assign PZ values to those variables.

Example:
Publics in automotive industry:
External Publics:

What segment of the population is most likely to request our automobile?
What is the financial demographic of our target customer?
Where do the majority of our target customers live?
Will they need special terms, financing, and incentives?

Internal Publics:

Can our service team handle the additional workload?
Do we have adequate sales channels (dealers) in that geographic area?
Has marketing analyzed competitive terms, financing, and incentives?
Are there enough autos available for demonstration?

All of these and more should be identified and plotted. Again, there are no hard and fast rules regarding the *PZ variables*. In fact the more you can identify the greater your chance of an accurate sales map. This sales map, or *PZ matrix* becomes your personal sales action plan; the direction that drives your daily planning as well as determining marketing, product positioning, training needs, etc.

The above matrix examples have hopefully clarified the concepts and embedded the PowerZone process. Now we're ready to apply the PZ principles to practical use!

DeFinaData:
The PowerZone Matrix becomes our overall plan and daily direction, leading to maximization of sales and ultimately to domination of the market niche.

3

Defining Power Zone Attributes

Now let's begin to look at *Power Zone variables* in terms of their attributes. You may be familiar with baseball bats. Louisville Slugger is a leading brand. Imagine that you lead a sales force whose main mission is to maximize sales of Louisville Sluggers.

What attributes immediately come to mind?
Hardwood, well balanced, aerodynamically designed, strong brand awareness.
Previously, we learned to assign *PZ values* from 1 to 5 to those *PZ variables* according to the most salient attributes.

In a *PowerZone Workshop* there might be active discussion over your choices. Have you validated the attributes to be PZ5 and PZ4? The members of your study group may differ greatly. Don't your competitors use hardwood? Aren't their bats just as well balanced? So what then may be the single one or two most compelling reasons that customers choose Louisville Sluggers?

Take a look at Louisville Slugger's webpage. What does the company say about the bats?

Very prominent are the words "history", "technology", and "players". A bat is a bat, right? But Louisville Sluggers are used by 60% of major league players as well as 70% of university baseball teams that won the collegiate World Series. It would be safe to assign a PZ5 value to the *PZ variable* "used by major leaguers!" That is why YOU want a Louisville Slugger!

Applying the *PowerZone* concept we'll take a look at just how other companies have arrived at the *PZ values* for their product thereby solidifying the PZ process in your own mind. To help focus you even more on *PZ mapping*, the eventual result of *PowerZoning* (yes, it can be used as a verb), I've engaged a technique utilizing actual interviews with some diverse companies who dominate their particular niche using *PowerZone* principles.

As the interviews unfold, we'll pause to highlight *PZ variables* and assign *PZ values* in much the same method as you might do to create your own *PZ strategy* or map. One excellent way to arrive at your product's PZ is to create a mock interview for your own product.

Questions might be:

What are the problems that this product solves?

PZ5_____

PZ4_____

PZ3_____

PZ2_____

PZ1_____

What competitor's products also could solve these problems?

PZ5_____

PZ4_____

PZ3_____

PZ2_____

PZ1_____

At what price would this product move rapidly to the customer?

PZ5_____

PZ4_____

PZ3_____

PZ2_____

PZ1_____

The PowerZone Sales System

What is the optimum price for us in terms of margin and profitability?

PZ5_____

PZ4_____

PZ3_____

PZ2_____

PZ1_____

Which category of our resellers, dealers, channel part-ners are best suited to sell this?

PZ5_____

PZ4_____

PZ3_____

PZ2_____

PZ1_____

Who are our most qualified salespeople?

PZ5_____

PZ4_____

PZ3_____

PZ2_____

PZ1_____

As the group continues to discuss, many more PZ variables will arise as a result of this interviewing process. Risks are minimized when this step is thoroughly developed.

DeFinaData:
PowerZoning is a process that culminates in the creation of the *PZ strategy*, this becomes the direction for the individual or company that leads to market niche dominance.

To illustrate the effectiveness of the PZ interview technique, I conducted actual interviews with companies that have achieved dominant or significant market share in their particular category space. Before the interview, the company spokesperson or executive was provided with *PowerZone* text and in some cases additional personal consultation.

I'll highlight sections of the interview text that yielded *PZ variables* or attributes and we'll plot them in a *PZ matrix*.

PowerZone Case Study Interview

Paul Reed Smith Guitars
Annapolis, MD

In the mid eighties, the major guitar manufacturers were producing decent quality product but arguably nothing on the scale of what they produced during the guitar industry's "golden years"- the fifties and sixties.

Most of the original 1950's and 1960's guitar models from prominent makers were selling for as much as twenty to forty times more than their original prices to musicians and collectors that appreciated the fine wood, workmanship, feel, and sound produced on these instruments from a classic era. The fact that demand had greatly challenged the ability of major manufacturers to maintain quality *and* continue mass production of these fine instruments led a young artisan and gifted guitar repairman; Paul Reed Smith, to make a guitar for himself modeled after one of his favorites from the late fifties. Having worked on hundreds of these vintage pieces as a repairperson, Paul Smith experienced first hand the construction and material that made these instruments so special.

After building a few guitars which directly copied the classic designs Paul embarked on a mission to combine the best attributes of these fine classics into a new guitar with the addition of his own proprietary improvements upon the revered but yet imperfect legacy designs. In fact, many guitar aficionados and prominent rock stars argue that PRS guitars have even exceeded those from the golden era.

Determined to share his wonderful prototypes with the professional guitarists of nationally touring rock bands,

Paul worked his way backstage at major concerts where he would hand his prototype guitar to a top guitarist in hopes of having them order one for use on stage. Amazingly the deal was "try this guitar, if you like it pay me for it" I spent considerable time discussing *Power-Zone* concepts with Paul Reed Smith and have spoken with him at length about the company's *PowerZones* and PRS Guitars. Paul was particularly poignant in a published interview which really focused on PRS Guitars' *PowerZones* but not in an overt "features and benefits" way. This is a good exercise in analyzing thoughts and nuances from an interview in order to capture essential *PowerZones*. I've included the abridged text of the interview below. Since we're *PowerZoning*, I've underlined and emboldened those PZ attributes pertinent to our study.

PRS Guitars Interview, Reprinted with permission from *Music and Sound Retailer,* (M&SR) *Vol.26*, No. 7, July 15, 2009

M&SR: Take us into the life of Paul Reed Smith. What's your typical day like? How do you get everything done?

Paul Reed Smith: It is very busy but every day is different. What is interesting for me is that **I am a guitar maker**, but the business does call for me to do other things. I don't get it all done…it is really never ending… but I do try to tend to the things that are most important for the company: our **dealers, distributors, customers, employees** and of course, **our guitars**. It also helps that I truly love what I do…and I get to work with a **great team** like Joe Knaggs in *Private Stock*, Steve Fischer in *Acoustics*, and Doug Sewell in *Amps*... and many, many others. Theses people know I will literally give them the shirt off my back in **appreciation** for all they do.

M&SR: *PRS* will be celebrating its 25th anniversary in 2010, only a few months away. Can you believe it's almost 25 years since the business began?

Smith: Yes...I can believe it...and we have very big plans. I look in the mirror and my hair is white. I have learned and experienced so much in that time. The funny thing about it is that the **business is the same except for the size.** We still put out **high quality** instruments, we are still **looking for ways to improve them**, and we still have the **passion and love** to turn out **magic guitars**. All of these things we have had right from the beginning and still have them today...we just have more people doing it. I am very proud of our products and the **people who make them**, because I know they all have the same love I do. It's been a long and fruitful road...Someone once told me the best way to look forward is to look in the rearview mirror and I totally believe that, so that's what I have been doing for the past 25 years.

M&SR: Some dealers have told us it is very difficult to sell **$2,000+ guitars** in this market. Have you heard the same thing? If so, what can you tell the dealers to help them to better sell those products?

Smith: We are being affected way less than a lot of other manufacturers. If someone thinks the instrument will stand **the test of time**, and it's **worth it**, those instruments will sell. It is not an uncommon experience…when a house is on fire that the homeowner is begging the fireman to go back in and get their *PRS*. I have heard the story numerous times…it is a really good sign.

M&SR: What's one thing about *PRS* the company that you'd like everyone to know?

Smith: I think there are a large number of **very skilled people** working here. Because we don't have a lot of other guitar makers in this state they can go work for; we try to provide a **place for them to work for a very long time**. Everyone who knows me is aware I think the world of them. They are a pleasure to be around. The **guitar I play** comes right off the line. Try one that we've recently shipped and you'll see what I mean.

There are **scores of improvements**. I am pulling guitars out of cases and the sound is wonderful. There is no way to explain it unless you try it.

M&SR: What measures can you take or have you taken to make sure you're even stronger when the economic recovery hits its stride?

Smith: We're continually **improving the sound** of our products…the 1957/2008 pickup is one example of this...though it wasn't developed as a protective measure. **Innovation** is a constant part of the *PRS* mission...and that gives us the strength to continue to grow. We also have **new product lines** and team members in place like Steve Fischer in Acoustics and Doug Sewell in Amps. This type of product diversification will help us as will having the best people on our team. **END**

As you have no doubt surmised, sometimes you need to dig to find the essential PZ attributes when *PowerZoning*. All interviews or even *PZ Workshops* will not instantly yield identifiable *PowerZones*. Careful study and validation is key.

Study the emboldened and underlined phrases above. Some *PZ Attributes* are clearly features but another subtle but powerful attribute emerges. One of *PRS Guitar's* greatest *PowerZones* is Paul himself! Culture can be a significant PZ advantage in a business largely dependant upon artisans. These people can see the result of their art each day. Paul Smith clearly understands and addresses this through his focus on people and the underlying culture at *PRS*.

A PowerZone Matrix based on the above may look like this:

PowerZone Matrix "*Paul Reed Smith Guitars*"

	Insignificant	Low Sig-nificance	Marginal	Secondary	Primary
PZ Variable	**PZ1**	**PZ2**	**PZ3**	**PZ4**	**PZ5**
Construction	Price			Reliability Hardware	Build Quality Material/wood
Sound			High end	Good overall	Excellent Humbucker
Luthier					Paul Smith visionary
Finish					Highest Quality
Price	Mass market				Price/quality

PRS Guitars is aimed at the high end of the market. PZ variables in this category include many items that yield quality at the "best in class" level. If you were *PowerZoning* the channel partners in this example, you probably would conclude that mass merchandisers would not be the best outlet for these guitars. Price is almost always directly related to value. The *PRS* clientele would be sophisticated enough to determine the relative quality of materials, finish and construction. This does not indicate that the guitars would appeal to all high end customers. Consider the PZ attribute, "sound". This is a subjective attribute but clearly indicates that some players, although sophisticated, do not desire the tone of a *PRS* but prefer another sound. This may be a PZ3 for *PRS* but a PZ5 for a competitor. PZ Matrix analysis can be a useful tool in competitive studies.

Miele is a German manufacturer of high quality domestic appliances and machines for commercial applications. The company was founded more than 108 years ago in 1899 by Carl Miele and Reinhard Zinkann and has always been a family-owned, family-run company.

Miele aims to manufacture the highest-quality domestic appliances and commercial equipment in the world and to be seen by markets worldwide as providing an absolutely top-class household product.

In the words of *Miele's* founding fathers, Carl Miele and Reinhard Zinkann, "Success is only possible in the long term if one is totally and utterly convinced of the quality of one's products." Therefore, continuous innovation is the foundation of their business success.

The customer, for whom the company provides first-class products and services, is at the center of attention. Thanks to this company philosophy which focuses on the dynamic development of quality and technology, the *Miele* brand is now identified with unsurpassed product quality.

Thomas J. Foy is National Training Manager responsible for sales, product training, dealer training, and internal departmental training. He is also tasked with, Architect and Design channels, client, and civic events in the company's headquarters gallery. I spoke with Mr. Foy at *Miele Corporation of America* headquarters.

1) **Author**: What makes *Miele* products so special?

Tom Foy: First and foremost, it is our commitment to **quality**. *Miele* is a 110-year old family owned business, which sells products in over 60 countries worldwide. We excel in development, technology, **ease of use**, **environmental impact**, longevity and **durability**. We insist on unparalleled quality in every aspect of every product we develop and manufacture. In fact, **we make about 85 to 90%** of all the materials that go into our products, including our own electronics. This insures us quality control and testing capabilities that simply stated, **don't exist in the appliance industry**.

We also test our products in a variety of ways—as they are being developed, during the manufacturing process, and at the end of the production line, every product is tested. In fact, *Miele* products are designed and tested to **last 20 years**. This is unique to the appliance industry.

We are also environmentally driven. We offer **lower water and energy use** than other brands. We are vertically integrated, which allows us to manufacture most of our parts and products with a relatively small carbon footprint. And, because of our 20 year life-span on products, we have less impact on natural resources over time.

And having the family name on the products is a source of pride and our adherence to quality. This is supported by our company motto, "*Immer Besser.*" The literal translation is "forever better."

2) **Author:** What is the first thing you'd want me to know if I was hovering around a *Miele* oven in one of your showrooms?

TF: Well, first of all, before I'd offer any information to you, I'd want to know more about **your needs**. What brought you into our Showroom? How did you hear about us? What are you trying to accomplish? These are questions that I would need to ask, to better understand your thoughts, and more importantly your feelings about our products in relation to your needs. From there, based on your answers I could address only those aspects that were most important to you. For example, if you told me you were remodeling your kitchen, I'd like to know about the project and how our oven can affect the lifestyle change you're attempting to make in your kitchen.

Or, if you simply needed a replacement oven, because yours had died, I'd like to know what you liked about your previous oven, but more importantly, what you didn't like?

That way, we could address only those features and benefits that were most relevant to your needs. Whether it was quality, performance, longevity, ease of use, or simply

status, *Miele* can offer our client any aspect that drives their desire.

3)   **Author:** What would you want to know about me if I happened to be in your store (showroom)?

TF: I'd want to get to know what drives your decision making. I'd like to know about your wants, needs, aspirations, and desires. Buying is an emotional business.

Too often buying experiences go bad for consumers because we, as sales professionals, don't address the **emotional aspect** of the process. For example, most people do research prior to making a major purchase. **They search the internet**. They ask family and friends whose opinion they trust. They **review consumer magazines**.

They do the research for a variety of reasons—they don't want to appear uninformed, they want to make a sound choice, or they don't want to be taken advantage of or be sold the wrong product.

This process comes with stress, tension, apprehension, and sometimes even fear. However, the other end of that emotional spectrum is where the positive effects can occur. But they can only occur once the client feels comfortable and trusts your intentions to guide and advise them. Then, and only then, can they discuss the emotional values that are driving their search for our products.

4)   **Author:** Why are *Miele* products so **expensive**?

TF: All products are not alike. All dishwashers do not yield the same results. All ovens perform differently. All refrigerators offer different features. Premium products offer additional value that clients are seeking. When one can uncover the value statements that drive a clients decision making process, then price becomes less of a factor in the sales event. *Miele* is a product that offers many values to a client, whether it is **performance,** results, **longevity**, latest **technology, aesthetics, ease of use,** or the aforementioned quality. Premium products come at a different price, but also offer significant additional values for the client.

5)   **Author:** What problems will a *Miele* oven solve?

TF: A Miele oven, or any other *Miele* product for that matter, will yield **improved results**, provide the latest technology, be **easy to use**, and provide exceptional aesthetics, workmanship, and **quality**. But, since you asked about ovens, the *Miele MasterChef* Ovens will allow anyone from the novice to gourmet to achieve exceptional results. For the novice, we have a **food-driven menu** that will select the appropriate cooking application based on the items selected, as well as the desired doneness. It will also **notify you** *when* the item is done.

And, for the novice, they can even **store 30 of their most used recipes**, for a one touch application. For the gourmet, who typically knows their way around an oven, they can **manually select** a cooking application—

convection bake, convection roast, broil—and modify it to their desires, in effect, customize it to their particular cooking style.

6) **Author:** Why don't you sell your products at a large **chain store?**

TF: *Miele*, as a family business, built its company culture on partnering with independent dealers for over 110 years. It is a tradition that still continues today. It is our goal to partner with people and businesses who are interested in quality, and all the other attributes that *Miele* offers as a **premium product**. We could certainly take a mass market approach to our business. But, we feel that the perception and reality of who we are in the premium spectrum could be compromised. Our **partnership with independents** has served us well, in terms of commitment *to* our dealer base, as well as commitment *from* our dealer base. It has also allowed us to provide **greater support** to our independent dealers from our sales force, training force, and marketing groups.

For *Miele*, it is not simply about selling numbers…it is about selling the finest quality premium products on the planet. It is also a constant commitment to drive technology, innovation and quality control, so that our dealers are delivering the finest products to their clients. **END**

A *PowerZone Matrix* based on the above may look like this:

The PowerZone Sales System

*PowerZone Matrix "**MIELE**"*

	Insig-nificant	Low Signifi-cance	Mar-ginal	Second-ary	Primary
PZ Variable	**PZ I**	**PZ2**	**PZ3**	**PZ4**	**PZ5**
Construc-tion					Durable Reliable
Environment					Low Envi-ronmental Impact
Ease of Use	Portable				Food Driven Menu
Availability	Chain Stores			Contractors	Independent Dealers
Price	Bargain				Quality/Price

Consider the *Miele* example and populate the matrix to yield your own conclusions. How would you sell *Miele* products if you worked for the company? Which specific customers would you target? How would you approach them?

4

Building YOUR PowerZone Matrix

Consider the PZ matrix below:
PowerZone Matrix "Security Cameras"

	Insignificant	Low Significance	Marginal Significance	Secondary PowerZone	Primary PowerZone
PZ Variable	**PZ1**	**PZ2**	**PZ3**	**PZ4**	**PZ5**
Features	Price	connectivity	Day/Night Capable	Reliability	Picture Quality
Total cost of Ownership					X
Salesperson.	Abramson	Green	Patel	Masterson	Mace
Application	Churches and Synagogues	C-Stores	Casinos	School Playgrounds	Parking Lots

We've identified the pertinent variables in the far left column and then assigned a PZ value in subsequent columns from left to right. Notice that in the case of "total cost of ownership" we've place an "X" to denote that relative to other options our solution provides the best long term value for the customer. PZ values can have ranking numbers or simply be scaled as in the TCO example.

As previously mentioned, the PZ process works best when teams are engaged. You may want to create your own PZ matrix but I remind you to validate your assumptions, and, discuss your plan with your sales manager.

Begin by identifying the PZ variables of your primary product or service. If you handle many products then you could plot them as a category, an example from the pharmaceutical industry; "pain inhibitors" rather than "Provactin B".

A spreadsheet software application is useful in this stage. You should identify as many PZ variables as possible. This is where the team approach can significantly help to validate assumptions and to minimize risk.

PowerZone Matrix "My Product or Service"

	Insignificant	Low Significance	Marginal	Secondary	Primary
PZ Variable	**PZ1**	**PZ2**	**PZ3**	**PZ4**	**PZ5**

In the far left column list as many PZ variables as you can. The most important attributes will surface quickly while the less apparent ones will develop through the process. It may help to refer to marketing literature or PR information that already exists. It would be helpful to create an electronic spreadsheet so that numerous attributes or variables can be plotted and *PowerZoned*.

DeFina Data:
Beware; your existing marketing message may not necessarily be highlighting your *PowerZones*!

Don't forget the vital internal and external *publics* that may affect your sales. Is your logistics team (internal public) capable of instant shipping if that was identified as a PZ5 for the market? Will the general population (external public) accept orange flavored coated aspirin?

The PowerZone Sales System

Think in terms of selling your product or service. What attributes would you focus on in a sales presentation? Are these your primary or secondary *PowerZones*? Which insignificant *PowerZones* should you avoid? Your product will have some weakness for the market or application you are selling into. This may be a competitor's *PowerZone*!

Be prepared to address these weaknesses and remember to concentrate on your own PZ 4 and PZ5 attributes.

5

PowerZoning your Competitors!

Your product or service exists in a dynamic market, one that is likely to change over time. As you incorporate *PowerZones* into your daily regimen you'll need to be constantly aware of your competitor's strategy. You can be sure that they'll be watching your success and implementing countermeasures. And, PowerZoning you and your product!

In this chapter we'll *PowerZone* the competition utilizing the same interviewing methodology from previous chapters. Will you actually interview your competitor? Not likely. But you will virtually interview them and glean *PowerZone* attributes and values. This technique will reveal much about their strengths and allow you to exploit their weaknesses.

DeFinaData:
Any good business will draw competitors who inevitably find ways to out price, out feature, and out sell. Be prepared by *PowerZoning* the competition regularly then adjust your strategy accordingly.

In the *PowerZone Matrix*, we will plot our competitors' *PowerZones*. The idea is to avoid *their* PZ while focusing on our own. It is vital that you thoroughly understand exactly what your competitors' value propositions are likely to be and plan to counter them with your own PZ strategy.

Example: Consider that you are approaching a potential customer in a surveillance application for a commercial parking lot in NYC. Assuming that your product is similarly priced, you begin by plotting the two or three *most* compelling reasons that your product *solves* your customers' problem.

Do this *before* the sales call! At this point make some general assumptions of the customer's problem. Validate these during the customer visit.

Example: Tarlowe WV-459 Dome Camera

1) (PZ5) Reliable construction, sets the industry standard

2) (PZ5) Great day/night performance

3) (PZ4) Heater/Blower enclosed, internal moisture elimination

Now do the same for the competitor whose value proposition most closely matches yours:

Example: Sondog XY-101 Dome Camera

    4)   (PZ5) Connectivity to the internet

    5)   (PZ5) Great day/night performance

    6)   (PZ4) Heater/Blower enclosed, internal moisture elimination

During the actual sales call your prospect states:

"I've heard a lot about the Sondog XY-101 camera, it appears well suited to my situation"

Through *PowerZoning,* you are well aware that Sondog's camera, although good, cannot produce images in low lighting conditions; an easily demonstrable PZ attribute you identified as vital to this type of customer.

You could confidently respond:

"Sondog is a very good company; I think we have developed some significant technological benefits that can solve your problems better. Please allow me to show you the images our camera produces in low light."

Then hit them with your company's PowerZones!

<u>DefinaData:</u>

Never speak poorly or disrespectfully about your competitor, rather, focus on your PowerZones to win the business!

We all wish that we could sell in an environment where there are no competitors but the point is to determine a strategy to dominate within that environment.

Pz+A=D   PowerZones+Alignment =Domination of Niche

Accept the fact that people shop, compare prices, check the internet, research, test, and ask for testimonials. Be prepared to position your product in terms of those *PowerZones* that best address the key buying decisions. And, understand your competitor's *PowerZones*. Avoid their PZ5's, and PZ4's while attacking at their PZ3's, 2's, and 1's.

Fill in the blanks on this simple chart to help you plot competition, then place these on an electronic spreadsheet based PZ Matrix for your competitors:

Number One Competitor_____

PZ5 product   _____

PZ4 product   _____

PZ3 product   _____

PZ2 product   _____

PZ1 product   _____

Do the same for the number two and three nearest competitors to your product or service.

Number Two Competitor_____
PZ5 product _____
PZ4 product _____
PZ3 product _____
PZ2 product _____
PZ1 product _____

Number Three Competitor_____
PZ5 product _____
PZ4 product _____
PZ3 product _____
PZ2 product _____
PZ1 product _____

You can also use the interviewing technique. Here are some sample questions that pertain to nearly every industry. Think of these in terms of BOTH your company as well as your main competitors'. Your PZ Team should be able to add more to this list.

1)   What are the 3 most compelling features of my product?
1A) My competitor's product?

2)   What are the key attributes of the typical buyer (personal or application)?

3) What is the best method (direct/indirect/ other) or channel (dealer/distributor/other) to reach or inform the buyer about my product?

4) Where can my customer learn about my product?

5) Who are the people influencing the decision to purchase? (we can assign a *PZ value* to these)

6) Does the target customer have sufficient funding allocated for this fiscal year?

7) Will the target customer pass my company's credit criteria? (an *internal public*)

8) Can the factory produce sufficient quantity?

DeFinaData:
Here is a classic and basic way to qualify a prospect:
BART
Does the prospect have Budget? Authority to decide? Responsibility for the purchase? Is this the correct Timing for the prospect?

From the virtual interview exercise identify the key *PZ variables* that you'll most likely encounter in a competitive situation. If "after sales service" is an example, assign a *PZ value* to it for each competitor. Determine at least three *PZ variables* for each competitor and assign the *PZ value* plotting these on your competitive PZ Matrix. We'll use your number one competitor; Sondog Manufacturing as a benchmark.

PowerZone Matrix "Security Cameras" **Competitor: Sondog Manufacturing**

	Insignificant	Low Significance	Marginal Significance	Secondary PowerZone	Primary PowerZone
PZ Variable	**PZ1**	**PZ2**	**PZ3**	**PZ4**	**PZ5**
Features	Low light	High Resolution	Day/Night Capable	Reliability	Price
After sales Service		X			
Technical Sales force	X				

A simple conclusion about *Sondog Manufacturing* is that they sell based on price and offer little after sale support. Also, their salespeople are likely to be order takers rather than technically capable. This does not infer that *Sondog* is not a well run and profitable competitor. It may mean that you should not approach competing with *Sondog* based on pricing (their PZ5) and that you can probably compete best with product that requires highly technical sales staff and excellent after sales support:

Competitive studies such as exemplified above should be undertaken with great attention to detail and with appropriate validation. Within an industry, there are likely to be very similar *PZ variables*. The key is to identify those and then accurately assign *PZ values*.

Use the team or *PowerZone Workshop* approach to help assemble and align the PZ variables. The initial effort may take considerable time but a well constructed PZ Matrix can be easily maintained. The sales increase and morale boost to the team will be worth the effort!

DefinaData:
Essential to effective *PowerZoning* is the simultaneous and continual assessment of your competitors.

Continue to update the PZ matrix as you proceed throughout the actual sales process. Information should be gathered, validated and plotted regularly.

Again, during a sales call, ask questions! One of my favorite approaches is to ask a question based on information gathered as I *listened* to the customer state their problem early on in the sales call. This customer indicated that an inordinate amount of inventory was unaccounted for each month and that employee theft was suspected. I asked:

Do you think our proposed solution will help stop theft in the warehouse?

That may sound apprehensive but if the prospect affirms your proposal by responding:

"I think it will help. I like the fact your camera is good in low light. We believe most of the pilferage occurs after hours when lights are dimmed to conserve energy".

She is selling herself based on your *PowerZones!* The objective is to keep *her* talking and hopefully to understand what problem of *hers* your product will solve.

This is also a prime opportunity to determine exactly which competitor has been approaching your prospect. The answer to your probing question might lead right to your competitor! Remember that *PowerZoning* is a continuous process.

Perhaps the response is:

"Your product looks good but the Sondog camera has an internet connection".

Don't panic. By now you have a good grasp of *PowerZoning* so you can answer confidently since you've *Power-Zoned* the competitor prior to the sales call. Right?

Your response might be:
"The Sondog is a good camera. Is internet connectivity essential to solving your problem? You've told me that your security guards monitor from a central office and that most of the pilferage occurs at night. You'll need a camera that works well in dimly lit situations allowing your guards to clearly see any suspicious activity."

Your prospect, by her own words, is being redirected back to your *PowerZones!*

Internet connection would be nice to have but the main problem PZ5 (yes, you can approach a problem by *PowerZoning*!) is not addressed by connectivity but rather by seeing images in low light, a problem nicely solved by your camera.

6

Organization of the PowerZone Sales Effort

We've spent considerable time understanding and applying the principle of *PowerZones* in product, services, and people. Now we must organize the sales effort utilizing our *PowerZone Matrix* aligning our PZ5, PZ4 attributes to dominate in our market niche.

The concept of PZ values leads us to the realization that some of our products are potentially market leaders while the remainder may be marginal. This does not imply that PZ2's and PZ1's cannot be sold; rather, we must develop alternate strategies for those products.

Consider products in your line that may range from "sophisticated" to "commodity". In the electronics field we could use examples like a camera surveillance system for a casino utilizing hundreds of cameras aimed at gaming tables-connected to a central command center. One can easily imagine a room with racks of monitors viewed by security personnel. Intuition tells us that many people were involved in the security assessment, system design, installation, and maintenance.

A PZ Matrix for this example probably would include PZ Attributes such as engineering experience, image quality, CAD capability, after sales support, and relationship with casino procurement people.

The same company manufactures a $99 camera that can be used by any consumer to monitor the rooms of a vacation home- accessing and viewing the images from a laptop computer connected to the internet.

By definition, this camera would need to be simple, easily installed by the consumer, and available in places where the consumer would most likely encounter such a camera. The image quality would be such that a user could see that a garage door was left open or that an intruder was in the house. Details like license plate numbers could not be seen and the intruders face would not be easily discernable. Imagine a PZ matrix for this "commodity" product. PZ attributes like price, web sales, simple operation, and easy installation-would appear in the PZ5 and PZ4 columns while image quality, face to face selling, engineering support, would appear under PZ1 and PZ2 columns.

Organization of the sales effort involves careful study through *PowerZoning* and then ***aligning*** your sales force or sales plan to maximize sales in that market for the particular product.

In the case of the "sophisticated" example of casino security, the alignment of PZ5's and PZ4s will ultimately dictate the requirement for sales engineers and thus face to face contact over several months. Obviously the telemarketing or retail sales approach would fail. Relationships would be key here. Profit margins would have to be considerable in order to cover cost of systems design as well as pre and post sales support.

Nuances within the market need to be considered. If we are particularly adept (based on our PZ matrix) at selling into the Biloxi market rather than Las Vegas (perhaps our relationship is a PZ5 for Biloxi and a PZ3 for Las Vegas), then we would begin by prioritizing those casinos in Biloxi that are near the end of useful life on their existing systems, brand new casinos, or replacing existing cameras with newer technology.

The PZ attributes for "sales person" would include names of sales engineers that enjoyed good relationships within Biloxi and had demonstrated success in the casino market.

DeFinaData:
Prioritizing opportunities based on a *PowerZone matrix* will provide a sales plan with the greatest chance for success. Likewise, compensation of the sales team should directly relate to the alignment of *PowerZones*.

In my experience, sales plans work best when we allow salespeople to be in front of customers for the majority of their selling time. Therefore, sales planning should be done through the PZ process *together* with the sales manager. What we're after is a well constructed PZ matrix that essentially becomes marching orders for the sales team. If they participated in the PZ process, then they'll welcome the idea of highly structured and organized method to selling that PZ provides-and they'll enjoy the benefits of increased sales.

It is my observation over many years that most salespeople struggle with the organization of the sales effort - becoming victims of "responsive selling", that is, responding to whatever opportunity or crisis appearing on any given day. This is NOT a directed, organized sales force!

We want the team to be calling on those prospects that have the highest probability of buying our solutions and avoiding those that are competitive PZ5s. Again, no hard and fast rules, we're just optimizing precious sales time. The competitor's PZ5s may be future customers but we need to be sure to dominate by maximizing our sales time and focusing effort in our PZ5 categories first. An inside sales support team or virtual support (internet sales) should be handling and fulfilling inquiries for products from PZ3, PZ2, and PZ1 customers, or, for products with small margins where high volume is needed.

7

Aligning PowerZones with your Marketing Message

Marketing should also be strongly considered and approached through *PowerZoning*. We can already sense what a PZ marketing matrix for the casino market example in the previous chapter might look like. Advertising, trade shows, web messaging would be aimed at capturing the attention of casinos but specifically in the Biloxi market. We would still want to stay in touch with Las Vegas opportunities but probably approach that market with a vastly different method.

In any event, *PowerZones* must be prominent in all communications, web pages, advertising, public relations, and press events. Take a moment to examine your own company's web page. What *PowerZones* are immediately apparent? Are there 'hot links", that is, can one click on the "high quality" icon or other phrase that links to a *PowerZone* based explanation? Web pages should be designed to sell products and services. If you worked for a major pharmaceutical company then your home page should highlight your most recent drugs or devices. An auto dealer should focus messaging on service, availability, or even price if it is a high volume-low margin dealer. Restaurants might show sources of fresh ingredients, a photo of a Tuscan countryside where olives for the spring salad are harvested.

What are the prominent *PowerZones* highlighted in the following advertisement?

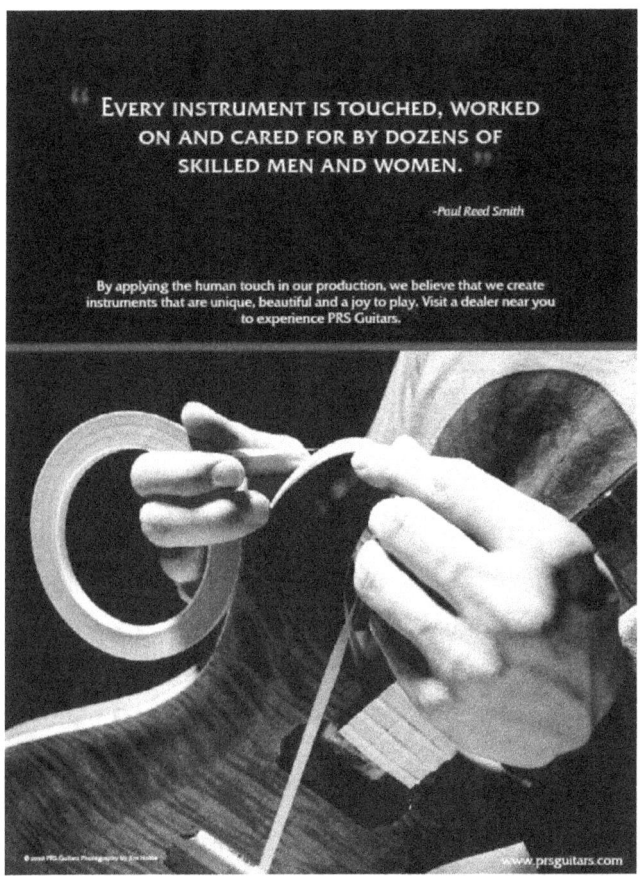

The preceding ad contains few words but the *Power-Zones* are quite clear and effective.

List the *PRS Guitars PowerZones* here:

PZ Attribute_____ PZ Value_____

PZ Attribute_____ PZ Value_____

PZ Attribute_____ PZ Value_____

PZ Attribute_____ PZ Value_____

PZ Attribute_____ PZ Value_____

See if yours match my own appearing below:
Your Comments on the above ad:

_____

_____

_____

_____

Author's list of the *PRS Guitars PowerZones*:

PZ Attribute	**Human Touch**	PZ Value	**5**
Z Attribute	**Joy to Play**	PZ Value	**5**
PZ Attribute	**Price**	PZ Value	**3**
PZ Attribute	**Construction**	PZ Value	**5**
PZ Attribute	**Paul Reed Smith**	PZ Value	**5**

Comments: These guitars are made by hand and by some incredibly good craftspeople. These are obvious since the ad focuses on *PRS* people as much as the guitars themselves.

Attributes such as "joy to play" are directly related to the "human touch" *PowerZone*. The most significant PZ in my mind is that the quote is from Paul Reed Smith himself.

This is an extremely significant *PowerZone* in that the founder of the company is still the company's chief visionary and designer.

In the same campaign, *PRS* used the following alternate ad with the same effect. Look for PZ5 and PZ4 especially, but notice how effective the ads can be when other PZ values are included.

The PowerZone Sales System

In a subtle way, this version of the PRS ad campaign alludes to competitor's PZ1 and PZ2, i.e., "it is nearly impossible to build a musical instrument that has a voice without love and care". Makes one think that other manufacturers that mass produce guitars may not have the "human touch" necessary to turn raw wood into instruments with a human attribute like "voice". A very powerful message and clearly a result of *PowerZoning* the competition.

In the next exercise, let's return to *Miele Corporation* and view examples of two advertisements. Again we'll compare notes on subsequent pages.

Frank P. De Fina

75

The above ads *PowerZones* are highly focused.

List the *Miele PowerZones* here:

PZ Attribute_____ PZ Value_____

PZ Attribute_____ PZ Value_____

PZ Attribute_____ PZ Value_____

PZ Attribute_____ PZ Value_____

PZ Attribute_____ PZ Value_____

See if yours match my own appearing below:

Comments on the above ad:

_____

_____

_____

_____

Author's List of the *Miele PowerZones*:

PZ Attribute **Longevity**   PZ Value **PZ4**

PZ Attribute **Clothes last longe** PZ Value **PZ5**

PZ Attribute **Valuable Clothes**   PZ Value **PZ5**

PZ Attribute _____   PZ Value ____

PZ Attribute _____   PZ Value ____

Comments on the above ad:

Most everyone expects a manufacturer to say that their washer lasts longer so we can assign a PZ4 here. The fact that *Miele* actually claims "up to 50% longer" is compelling-PZ5. But, the most astounding attribute is "valuable clothing" and the fact that a *Miele* washer assures "better care" and they'll "last longer". This clearly aims the brand at the high end consumer-one who will likely pay premium price for excellence.

The preceding analysis clearly links a company's marketing, positioning, and message to *PZ variables* and *PZ values* within the individual market space. These ads were probably created outside a typical *PowerZoning* process but the point of this entire book has been to create and then magnify, expedite, organize, implement a PZ strategy in a highly **organized and repeatable** process.

Carefully examine your own company's advertising and web statements. What connectivity is there to your product's *PowerZones*? If there is a clear PZ element and PZ identity to your ad then your company has a cohesive PZ strategy supported by messaging. If you see no connection to PZ principles then walk over to marketing and hand them this book!

A catchy ad with no connection to PZ strategy is a dead message. And, a salesperson without a plan can only react. As a *PowerZone* salesperson you will unlock the potential in your product, market and yourself. The concepts in this book should be constantly reviewed as a living text, one that can guide you throughout your sales career. I urge you to share *PowerZoning* with your colleagues and with sales management. A cohesive, strategically directed sales effort will lead to sustained success.

Enjoy the journey.

APPENDIX A

Attributes of *PowerZone* Salespeople:

1) PZ salespeople are always reachable, carry their fully charged cell phone at all times and check regularly for messages.

2) Dress appropriately for the occasion; check with coworkers or managers in advance of event, meeting, sales call.

3) Prepare wardrobe for the week according to schedule. Clean suits, blazers, spotless ties, well shined shoes, neatly pressed shirts.

4) Are always aware of sales targets for month, quarter, and year. Track progress regularly and can immediately respond to management questions such as; "Where are your sales for the month vs. plan? What is your plan to make budget this month? Quarter? Year?

5) Complete all sales reports, progress reports, expense reports when due. Best to update these in the evening, same day, when information is fresh.

APPENDIX A

6) Are always on time for appointments, leave plenty of time for unpredictable events like traffic, accidents, weather, etc. Always call en route if they are going to be late explaining reason for tardiness. Apologize and indicate ETA.

7) Expect the unexpected. Customers cancel at the last minute, boss wants to accompany you on a sales call, flights delayed or cancelled. Plan a contingency scenario where possible. If weather threatens the day of the important sales call, go there the day before.

8) Anticipate customer's questions and objections. Calmly and professionally refocus customer onto your PowerZones! Never bad mouth competitors.

9) Do not engage in office gossip! Do your job, don't bad mouth anyone. The person you bad mouth could be an important future colleague or the boss's nephew.

10) At business functions drink alcohol lightly if at all. You'll constantly be watched and assessed by peers, customers, management.

APPENDIX A

11) ORGANIZE! Plan your week in advance, preferably on the previous Friday. Plan you work, work your plan. Expect that unforeseen customer issues will arise. Plan sufficient time to address these. Be prepared to instantly show the plan to superiors.

12) Sell during selling hours! Try to do planning and reporting before 9am and after 5pm. Your selling time is limited use it wisely!

13) Get to the office early, avoid last minute rushing. Prepare for demonstrations well in advance and preferably set up the product previous day. Make sure everything works, you can operate demo equipment flawlessly, anticipate questions, steer the presentation towards your Power-Zones while avoiding competitor's PZ.

14) Make sure you have any cables, connectors, manuals, samples, presentations, sales literature neatly packed and labeled the day before a demonstration. You will not have a great deal of time on site so planning and prep are essential to smooth and effective demo.

APPENDIX A

15) Know your product and its operation inside and out. Study the manual; anticipate questions, again, position your product in terms of Power-Zones!

16) Be conversational but professional. Ask questions! Make sure that you can obtain some indication as to the customer's problem. You are there for one reason...to solve the customer's problem, then and only then, can you ask for an order! Customer should talk at least three times as much as you!

17) LISTEN! The customer will tell you a lot if you only let him. WAIT until he finishes his sentence and ONLY then begin your response. Avoid telling everything about your product immediately. Rather, respond with references to your product's *PowerZones* after a question or comment from the customer. Be patient.

18) Above all else do not be ARROGANT! This is surely the path to failure. Customers expect that you know your product but avoid correcting them or arguing. GENTLY steer them away from inaccurate perceptions and back to your *PowerZones*.

APPENDIX A

19) Respect your superiors even if they are wrong! Again, gently prove your point and NEVER correct your boss in public, at a company function, or, in front of a customer.

20) Avoid discussing company business in public. Do not work on confidential presentations where your computer can be viewed. Assume competitors are seated next to you, behind you, or in proximity to you. They frequently are!

APPENDIX B

How to Create an Accurate Sales Forecast

An essential part of any salesperson's job is to provide an accurate sales forecast to management. Forecasts are used by factories to plan production schedules, financial departments to ascertain cash flow or to meet requirements for funding, and by top management in strategic planning. So they are very important! Please take them seriously.

Here's the process:

Determine the run rate (regular and often unpredictable sales based on ongoing customer purchases) of your particular product over the last 3 months, 6 months, and one year. For instance, you sell 300 cases of MOM'S SAUCE each month on a regular basis but not to any one predictable customer. These are typically ordered as needed rather than on scheduled delivery basis. Run Rate sales may be a result of inside sales activity, advertised promotions, or spontaneous buys when a customer walks into the store. They happen regularly and the amount is based on sales history over time. You know with high probability that you'll sell 140 corned beef sandwiches each week because you've averaged that number for the last 6 months. Be careful to view any spikes in the run rate analysis such as the fact that two months ago you sold 300 sandwiches during the high school homecoming. If this occurs omit that exceptionally high month and use months that were more typical of historical sales. Carefully determine the average run rate. Is the last month's number close to the average for the last 6 months and last year? If so and there are no significant changes such as you lost your biggest customer, begin with this number.

Example:

Last 12 months average sales per month for Product **X**	**1200 units**
Last month's actual sales for Product **X**	**1159 units**
Last 6 month's average actual sales per month	**1204 units**

Conclusion: Run Rate is stable so let's start with 1200 as our basic forecast.

1) What factors in this month can positively or negatively affect sales?
   a) Government has cancelled their PO for this month 90 units.
   b) We quoted XACO Oil on new widget buy of 300, new customer.
   c) Bilcol X is on credit hold, 40 units, new customer
   d) MA Corp demo slated for last week of month, 500 units per month potential

If we take a closer look at item #1a we need to answer some fundamental questions. If the government has been a consistent buyer during the last year then this cancellation cannot be counted as run rate so we must deduct 90 units from 1200 run rate.

Next, XACO quote should be studied. What is probability of closing this month?

If it is 85% or greater based on *PowerZoning* (aren't you glad you read this far?), that is your PZ matrix indicates you have beat the competitors based on features, problem solving, price, service, you can assume closing this one so add 300 to the number.

CAUTION: New customers are unpredictable by definition, if you have past experience with this customer and they usually come through, great. If you have no prior dealings, I'd reduce the forecast on XACO to half so let's add 150 instead.

BILCO is on credit hold and they are new. March down to credit department and see if this is just a set up or system issue or if it is unlikely they will be credit approved.

Usually new customers take longer to get into the system. If credit folks indicate they feel uncomfortable offer to help. Call the customer and ask if they can make alternative payment arrangement or pay C.O.D. on the first few orders. If things appear resolvable add 40 units.

The PowerZone Sales System

MA Corp looks promising. You've been after them for years, PowerZoned in preparation for your sales presentation and nailed it. They gave strong indications of moving business to you from your competitor. So? Ok. Two things to watch with MA Corp.: they are a potential new customer and they are possibly switching from your competitor. Pay attention at this stage. Your competitor will not easily give up on a steady customer and is making counteroffers. Time to communicate with MA. Are there any further questions? When can you visit them to train their people on your product? Assume the sale and work on implementing.

Second issue with MA: it is the end of the month, new customer, taken from competitor.

I would think the likelihood of all things working out perfectly is questionable so best not to add 500 here. Revisit MA for next month's forecast based on more work needed to close. If your company requires forecasts in excess of one month you should list MA and assign a probability percentage on closing.

So here's our forecast:
Run Rate   =   1200
Government   -90
XACO   +150
BILCO   +40
MA   new

FORECAST = 1300

Risks: XACO may not buy 150, or BILCO may not be credit approved.

APPENDIX B

You're in the clear, right?   Only if your quota or sales budget is 1300 or less.   If your forecast yields a number significantly below budget there is another critical component to your forecast which must be added. COUNTERMEASURES and ACTION PLAN to achieve quota! That is, what will you do this month to reach the sales quota? What is your action plan? Also what are the "risks to forecast" that is, what may happen that will negatively affect the forecast? Risks must be minimized hence the focus on countermeasures and action plan.

If the above exercise produced a forecast of 950 instead of 1300 you are obligated to provide management with the precise action plan that will help you make up the shortfall of 350 units (1300 quota minus 950 forecast equals 350 shortfall).

This is not easy but we'll approach it systematically and using PowerZone principles.

We need 350 units.

Questions to consider:

Have all existing quotations been reviewed and followed up?
Using PowerZone charts, which PZ5 and PZ4 customers are most appropriate to contact assuming they can buy promptly?

What short term promotions can be run and who will implement?

Can the dollars be achieved through accessory sales to existing customers?

Can hot products be bundled with existing inventory to create compelling reasons to buy now?

Will credit department permit extended terms on larger orders to existing customers?

What advantages can you provide to new customers or recently quoted customers to buy this month? Additional training? Free accessories? Co-Op ad dollars?

APPENDIX C

Basic Math for Salespeople

You finally landed a great position in sales. Or, you've been working in sales for a few years and managed to dodge questions about markup, margin, growth percentages because you don't really understand them. OK. Admit it. Now let's learn the basic math formulas that every salesperson should understand.

PRICING BASICS:

Cost: What your company pays for the product. Also, *landed cost or cost or goods*   *aka* **COGS.**

Price: What the customer pays for the product. Also, *selling price* or *retail price*.

BASIC FORMULAS: Cost of Goods + Markup = **Retail Price**
Retail Price - Cost of Goods = **Markup**
Retail Price - Markup = **Cost of Goods (COGS)**
Contribution Margin = Total Sales - Variable Costs
COGS = Beginning Inventory + Purchases - Ending Inventory

APPENDIX C

Gross Margin = Total Sales - Cost of Goods

Gross Margin Return on Investment (GM-ROI)

GMROI = Gross Margin $ ÷ Average Inventory Cost

Inventory Turnover = Net Sales ÷ Average Retail Stock

Margin % = (Retail Price - Cost) ÷ Retail Price

Markup $ = Retail Price – Cost

Markup % = Markup Amount ÷ Retail Price

Net Sales = Gross Sales - Returns and Allowances

% Growth = Difference Between Two Figures ÷ Previous Figure

Sell-Through % = Units Sold ÷ Units Received

Decimal/Percentage Conversion: You need to understand how percentages are expressed in decimal and vice versa. **10% in decimal** is **.10** or 0.10. To change decimal to percentage just **move the decimal two spaces** to the right; **.30 is 30%.** The number **0.348 becomes 34.8%.**

Fractions in formulas: Whenever you encounter a fraction remember that the **top number** (numerator) is *DIVIDED* by the **bottom number** (denominator). So, the **fraction** ½ is actually 1 *divided* **by 2.** If you calculate this it **yields 0.50** which as a **percentage is 50%.**

APPENDIX C

Markup: defined as a percentage added to the cost to determine the selling price. If it **costs** you **$100** to make a weather radio and you want a **30%** markup what would the selling price be?

MARKUP FORMULA: Selling Price = Cost X (1+markup %)

We take the **cost of the radio; $100** and **multiply it times 1.30** (1+30% or 1+.30) to arrive at the **selling price of $130.00**. Our gross profit is $30.

Summary Calculation: $100 X 30%=$30
                                         $100+$30= $130 Sell-
                                         ing Price

Gross Margin: Also known as *contribution margin* indicates the percentage of sales dollars that are profit. **A 30% markup does NOT yield a 30% margin** as illustrated by the following formula which calculates gross margin percentage or GM.

GROSS MARGIN FORMULA:

GM Percentage = <u>Sales Revenue – Cost of Sales</u>
                              Sales Revenue

Using our weather radio example let's assume we sold exactly one radio at the **selling price of $130**. It **cost us $100** to make. **We subtract $100** (cost of sales) **from $130** (Sales Revenue) to **arrive at $30**. We **di-**

vide $30 by $130 yielding a **23% GM**. This means **that for each dollar of sales, $0.23 were left** to contribute towards operating costs and profit generation.

Summary Calculation: **$130-$100=$30**
                           $30/$130=23%   Gross Margin

APPENDIX C

Using Gross Margin to Calculate Retail or End-User Price:

If it **costs** you **$1000** to make a bottle of pain pills and your sales manager wants you to make a **35% gross margin** on the sale of each bottle what would the selling price need to be?

CALCULATING SELLING PRICE AT SPECIFIED GROSS MARGIN

FORMULA: Selling Price = $\dfrac{\text{Cost}}{100\% - \text{GM}\%}$

Taking our **cost of $1,000** and **dividing it by .65** (100%-35% = 65% or .65) we arrive at a **selling price of $1,538.46**.   If you recall your math days you could say that you divide the cost by the *reciprocal* percentage, that is, the difference between 100% and the intended GM percentage. For instance, the reciprocal of 25% is 75%.

Summary Calculation: $1,000 / (100%-35%)
                        $1,000 / (65%)
                        $1,000 / .65 = $1,538.46

Sales Growth or Decline vs. a previous period:

You are scheduled to meet with your boss who wants to discuss your sales territory as part of your yearly review.

The PowerZone Sales System

One of the items she will surely cover is sales growth for your customers vs. the same period last year. How do you quickly calculate sales growth?

APPENDIX C

Last year your **sales were $2,090,345**. This year for the *identical sales period* your territory **sales were $2,980,876**. What is the percentage growth (increase) vs. last year?

SALES GROWTH
FORMULA:
Percentage Increase = **Increased amount – <u>Original amount</u>**
Original amount

Using the above results we **subtract $2,090,345** (Original amount or last year's amount) **from $2,980,876** (Increased or this year's amount) yielding a **difference of $890,531** which is the amount your sales have *increased* this year. We then divide $890,531 by the original amount which is **$2,090,345** for a **result of 0.426 or 42.6%** expressed as a percentage increase. You would report this as **+42.6%** vs. previous year.

Summary
Calculation: $2,980,876 - $2.090, 345 = $890,531
$890,531 / $2,980,876 = 0.426
= +42.6% Growth

SALES DECLINE

FORMULA:

Percentage Increase = Increased amount −
<u>Original amount</u>
Original amount

APPENDIX C

What if sales had declined to $1,909,564 this year vs. last year? Same formula.

Calculate the **difference** of the two years (**subtract $1,909,564 from $2,090,345**) to obtain a **difference of $180,781**. Now **divide $180,781** by last year's sales of **$2,090,345** to learn that your territory has *decreased* by **0.086** or **8.6%.** You should express this as -8.6% or *negative growth* in your sales reports.

Summary
Calculation: $2,909,345 - $1,909,564 = $180,781
$180,781 / $2,980,876 = 0.086
= - 8.6% or Negative Growth

Another common request may be to raise or lower your prices by a specified percentage.

PRICE INCREASE

FORMULA: **Current Price x 1 + the percentage increase**

The folks from headquarters have announced a **5% increase** on certain models in the product line and have asked that you apply the increase immediately on new orders.
The current price of your lawn mowers is $459 and you need to apply a 5% increase.

The PowerZone Sales System

Using the formula above simply multiply the current price; **$459** times 1+5% (or 1+.05=1.05) which can be expressed as **$459 times 1.05** (.05 being the decimal equivalent of 5%). The increased price is $481.95

Summary calculation: $459 X 1.05 = $481.95

APPENDIX C

PRICE DECREASE / DISCOUNT

FORMULA: Current Price x (100% - the percentage discount)

In this example you are asked to discount your price by 7% in order to reflect changes in the marketplace. Your wool snuggle hats have been retailing for $15.95 and now need to be reduced for clearance

Using our formula we first calculate the *multiplier*, that is, the percentage we will apply in order to discount the hats. In this example, **100% minus 7%** produces our **multiplier of 93%.** This is the same as stating that our hats will be priced at **93% of the original price**. So, we **convert 93% into decimal; .93** and **multiply that times $15.95** to reach the **discounted price of $14.83**.

Summary calculation: **$15.95 X (100% - 7%)**
$15.95 X 93%
$15.95 X .93 = $14.83
Discounted Price

GLOSSARY

Glossary of Terms

Pz+A=D The *PowerZone formula* which translates to *PowerZone*+Alignment Equals Domination of a market niche.

PZ Variable AKA *PowerZone Variable* denoting an attribute of product, service, market, people, channel, etc. pertaining to or directly affecting the sales process.

PZ value The *PowerZone Value*, a numerical value which ranks the Strength of the PZ variable relative to its competition, market acceptance, most salient feature or most compelling solution for the targeted customer. High (PZ5) to Low (PZ1).

PZ Matrix *PowerZone Matrix* or *PZ action matrix*, the chart which plots all PZ attributes *PZ values* or other *PZ variables*. This becomes the individual salesperson's plan to maximize sales based on the *PowerZone* process.

PowerZoning verb which denotes the actual process of applying PZ concepts to a given situation.

GLOSSARY

PowerZone Workshop Organized, formal event which combines sales team individuals into a *Power-Zoning* environment, leading to creation of the *PowerZone Action Matrix*.

PowerZone Dilemma The concept that, in any given sales environment, some products sell well while others struggle or "sleep in the warehouse".

Primary PowerZone A products' or service's most compelling sales features or benefits.

Secondary PowerZone Strong product or service attribute that supports the solution provided by the *Primary PowerZone* but is not the most compelling attribute.

Internal Publics The people, departments, or functions within the company that affect, positively or negatively, the sales team's ability to efficiently sell products or services.

GLOSSARY

External Publics Market, customer, governmental, regulatory, or influential participants that may affect, positively or negatively, the ability to maximize sales.

PowerZone **Alignment** The essential process which positions the strongest attributes of products and services, matching them with salespeople, channels, marketing, and messaging-to create the fundamental sales plan driving the sales effort of the individual or organization.

PowerZone **Strategy** The result of the PZ process which stems from organizing and analyzing all variables for your product and your competitors'; assigning ranking values of importance- aligning the most powerful aspects of all variables into a cohesive and executable sales plan.

CONTACT the Author:

Email: Frank@powerzoneselling.com
Blog: blog.powerzoneselling.com
Web Page: www.powerzoneselling.com